Love

Compiled by -
S. Chander

ॐ

STEP UP STRINGS

Love

Compiled by :
S. Chander

First Published : 2003

© S. Chander

ISBN 81-242-0331-8

Published by :

INDIANA
BOOKS
For Crest Publishing House
G-2, 16 Ansari Road,
Darya Ganj, New Delhi - 110 002
326 0651, 326 0618
e-mail : sethidel@del6.vsnl.net.in

Printed by:
Saurabh Printers Pvt. Ltd.
A-16, Sector IV, NOIDA

ॐ

Introduction

It is hard to define love in words . For true love cannot be defined, it can only be experienced. It is the highest piece of composed music but you have to strain the ears of your soul to hear it. Most people experience love without noticing anything remarkable about it. This book is an effort to explain to all those who are on the threshold of finding love, that love will surely find them and to those who have already found it, ways to sustain it. There is a lot of focus on aspects such as commitment, faith, trust, honesty-all of which seem so trivial but are indispensible to a successful relationship. In the fast paced world of today, where love has got killed by lust and more than that, by the departure of men and women from their real selves, the meaning of love is very important to complete the circle of our existence. For all those people, who are not ready to make a compromise, who understand the

3

difference between loving somebody and using somebody, for them love is still alive. It is love that is perfect and pure, everything else is sheer desire. Love, would like you to believe in few things. Every human being who walks this earth comes with some part of the heart broken, that's why we are here. We are here to meet the other half of us, who is made to shed a tear only to see that smile flash across our face. We are born only once, we die once and we fall in love once. Everything else is a compromise, habit or simply a need. If it's love, you don't even have to find it, it will find you.

Once it finds you, it will make you patient and considerate. It will fill you up with all the goodness that you used to appreciate with a touch of envy in people. It will give you the power to endure the worst, only to make everything the best for the one whom you love. Finally, this book is an effort to comfort all those who have lost their faith in the power of love, that the love of finest quality still exists. It is still alive.

4

Everyone comes into the world with a
piece of the heart broken.
Believe in love, till you find the other
piece of your heart.
God has made that heart
that will someday be yours.

Don't wait for your partner to say 'I Love You'. Make a start yourself. The gesture will be appreciated.

The best way to love anything is to
realize that it might be lost.

၅၁ပ၃

Find a map of your city or a place close to
your home. Together, select an area the two
of you have seen. Now, set out on a driving
adventure to the site.

7

We've got this gift of love, but love is like a precious plant. You can't just accept it and leave it in the cupboard or just think it's going to get on by itself.
You've got to keep watering it. You've got to really look after it and nurture it.

8

Make the effort to be "findable" and you'll see that you will soon be "found".

The prudence of the best heads is often defeated by tenderness of the best hearts.

There are many persons ready to do what is right because in their hearts they know it is right. But they hesitate, waiting for the other person to make the first move.

Drive around with a "Just Married" sign on the back of your car. Enjoy the reactions.

෨෬

"We can do no great things, only small things with great love"- Mother Teresa.

Don't forget that a person's greatest emotional need is to feel appreciated.

Find a restaurant with unusual or foreign dishes on the menu. Agree to order only those dishes you don't understand or recognize. Have fun guessing and tasting the foods.

Although you may get hurt, love passionately and completely. It´s the only way to truly get the most out of love, life, and your relationships!

13

Listening is different from hearing. When a person truly listens they not only hear the words, but they know the emotion behind those words. Communication occurs when someone truly listens and not just hears the words.

14

Romance is a balance of two concepts:
1) Actions speak louder than words.
2) It's the thought that counts.

When we know to read our own hearts,
we acquire wisdom of the hearts of others.

15

To attract attractive people, you must be attractive. To attract powerful people, you must be powerful. To attract committed people, you must be committed. Instead of working on them, work on yourself. If you become, you can attract.

Locate two pay phones in view of each other.
Call the other phone until some passerby picks
up. When one answers, ask the person a
question. The right answer has an award of
twenty-five cents which can be found
in the coin return.

Find out what new book your partner wants
to read, and buy it for him/her. Then write
a personal note on the first page of the book
along with the date. It shows you
are paying attention to your partner's
wants, and also makes for a special memento.

The first duty of love is to listen.

Write your own love poem or love letter.
A well-crafted love letter will have your lover
sighing with satisfaction.
Love letters also make for treasured keepsake.

Do a "random act of kindness" for your
partner. Surprise them with something
that they'll never expect.

All happy, successful, long-term relationships
are built on trust. That's why
character is so important,
so build a character base and
you will be at the top.

20

*Create a special signal to say "I love you"
when in public. A whistle, or a unique
smile will let your love know you´re
thinking about him/her.*

*Make a conscious effort to give each other
time each day. It´s amazing how taking
time out for each other 5 or 6 times a day
for just a few minutes will enhance
your relationship.*

Young love is when you love someone because of what they do right. Mature love is when you love someone in spite of what they do wrong.

Discuss which name of affection you'd like your Love to call you, e.g. Honey, Handsome, Snookims. Now, together create a signal to be used in public to mean "I Love You," e.g. double-hand squeeze, wink, a jig. Go for a walk or out to dinner, and practice using both.

If the spark has died in your relationship, there are so many ways to make it glowing again. Remember what it was that brought you together and make an effort to relive some of that.

When the evening is over, the gentleman should see the lady to her door. It is not enough to simply drive up to her house and open the car door for her. He should walk her up to the door of her home and see that she is safely inside before he leaves. This gives the lady the feeling of being protected.

24

Give a lift to you and your Love's lace-up shoes.
Together, go on a shoelace shopping spree.
Consider ribbons or laces as an option.

If you don't understand or like what your
partner is doing, ask about it and why he
or she is doing it. And vice versa. Explore.
Talk. Don't assume.

25

Don't shut love out of your life by saying it's impossible to find it. The quickest way to receive love is to give it; the fastest way to lose love is to not hold on too tightly to it; and the best way to keep love is to give it wings.

You and your Love sit down and talk about what declarations or promises you want to make to each other on behalf of the relationship. When you both agree, write them down. If you're already married, update your vows and read them on your next anniversary.

There´s nothing more romantic than looking into your love´s eyes and seeing the love for you reflected there.

There's no particular thing that would attract a person to you. People are turned on due to different reasons. Some are even mentally triggered, and want someone who loves opera music, or loves reading science fiction, or loves birding.

Just because you're in love doesn't make
courtesy and politeness redundant.
In fact, being in love gives you all
the more reason to treat the
other with love and respect.

Always say please and thank you.
Say you're sorry when you do something
wrong, or even if you just hurt their feelings.

Many people have found soulmates who did not exactly match with their own background. Realize that there might be hurdles to overcome, but that together you can easily surmount them.

Being free of the chores and drudgery of home can give you the mental peace that you need. You need the time to be able to look at each other as playmates and lovers instead of simply chore-partners.

What does your spouse do that you really appreciate? Make your list and give it to him/her for your anniversary, or some other special day of your lives.

Looking for a "lifetime perfect partner" is too large a job to take on in one step. First, look for a fun person that you can spend time with. Concentrate on that one task. If you can find someone that you enjoy being with, and want to be with, then you can move on to subsequent steps.

SHE MIGHT BECOME MY LIFETIME PERFECT PARTNER!

32

*You cannot expect your partner to be sensitive
and understand exactly how you feel
about something unless you're able to
communicate to him or her how
you feel in the first place.*

*Practise consideration. Whatever
consideration you show to others,
show twice as much to your beloved.*

A man without ambition is dead.
A man with ambition but no love is dead.
A man with ambition and love for his
blessings here on earth is ever so alive.

Find a place where wild flowers grow,
and the two of you go collecting.

We are born once, we die once
and we love only once.

Sit down when you have a few hours of quiet time, and write down what qualities are really important to you in a mate.

*Find an offbeat restaurant the two of you
have never gone to and try a
new dining experience.*

*The consciousness of being loved
and loving brings warmth and comfort
to life that nothing else can fetch.*

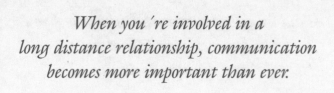

*When you´re involved in a
long distance relationship, communication
becomes more important than ever.*

38

During the next full moon,
play soft romantic music
and dance under the moonlight.

Love for man is but a part of his life,
for a woman it is her whole existence.

When your partner leaves you, don't forget to say 'Goodbye!' It's easy to get into the habit of walking out the door, but that last minute reminder that you do care will often carry subconsciously through the day. Give that last smile before the other parts of life take over.

40

Find a romantic poem book, then
read the poems out loud to each other.
Share your interpretations with each other.

&CB

Love never claims but only gives.
Love suffers, never resents, never avenges itself.

For a relationship not to stagnate, the persons within it must not stagnate. This may seem pretty straightforward, but a lot of couples learn this the hard way!

42

When two people love each other,
two against the world,
the two make their own world
and while the joy is shared, the sorrow split.

ॐ

The true reason of love is when you feel
that no one loves the way you do.

Don't leave celebrations for the memorable and major events. Celebrate when small things happen, and keep that aspect of specialness going. It can be a project completed at work, or a task at home finally done - grab some champagne and spend time together as a reward.

WE MUST CELEBRATE THE HOUSEHOLD CHORES YOU DID TODAY !!

*The cure for all ills in the world is love,
it is the divine vitality that produces
and restores life. It gives each one of
us the power to work miracles.*

*Love does not and will not support
people who want to find it at different
places with different people.*

Look up in the sky at night. Pick out a star. Call her and tell her to look out her window. Describe to her how to find the star you're looking at. Tell her that every time you look at the star, you'll think of her, and you'll make a wish. Tell her to think about you whenever she looks at the star, and to also make a wish. Chances are, you'll both end up wishing for the same thing.

Love knows no age, love luckily knows responsibility.

We love only once. Anything else is only habit, compromise, settlement.

When your lover has to go away on a trip for a few days, tuck a little surprise into his or her bag for each day of the trip.
It can be as simple as a pack of cards or a silly little toy. Be sure to wrap them up individually. Think of them as stocking stuffers. It will help him or her to ease the loneliness of being apart.

WITH LOVE FROM YOUR DARLING

A good sense of humour adds
spice to a romance.

Men always want to be a woman's first love.
That is their clumsy vanity. Women
have a more subtle instinct about things:
What they like is to be a man's last romance.

True love is like a ghost, which everybody talks about but very few have seen.

Romance lives by repetition, and repetition
converts an appetite into an art.
Besides, each tune one loves is the only tune
one has loved. Difference of object does not
alter singleness of passion.

The pleasure of love is in loving.
We are happier in the passion we feel
than in that which we arouse.

Many couples build fun into their routines.
Once a week, they grab the Sunday paper
and spend the morning working on the
crossword puzzle together. It´s quiet time,
part of their normal schedule,
that involves the two jointly having fun.
Give it a try!

Rent and watch the first movie
you saw together.

Admiration and desire
- both these are centered in love.

Find out what your sweetheart's wildest fantasy is; whether its joining the mile-high club, or climbing a mountain.
If it's something you're comfortable doing, do it! Even if it's expensive save up and surprise her--it will mean even more!

To love one who loves you,
to admire one who admires you,
to be the idol of one's idol,
is exceeding the limit of human joy.

Nothing is serious except passion.
The intellect is not a serious thing,
and never has been. It is only an instrument
on which one plays.

Usually, reliving the past is seen as a negative thing.
Now you can make it into something that enhances and strengthens your relationships:
Read old love letters to each other,
visit the venue of your first date, or better still,
recreate your first date.

*Love diminishes the delicacy of women
and increases that of men.*

*A man reserves his greatest and deepest love
not for the woman in whose company he
finds himself electrified and kindled
but for that one in whose company he
may feel tenderly drowsy.*

*Often the beauty we see in our loved ones
is difficult to describe...
Why not show them what you see?*

What a silly thing love is! It is not half as useful as logic, for it does not prove anything and it is always telling things that are not going to happen, and making one believe things that are not true.

But love is blind, and lovers cannot see the petty follies that they themselves commit.

One key trait that researchers find in just about every long-lasting couple is a good sense of humour. If the couple can laugh about things that go wrong, and enjoy life even when it's not perfect, that gives them the resilience to weather life's ups and downs.

*If one really loves a woman, all
other women in the world become
absolutely meaningless.*

*Romance should never begin with sentiment.
It should begin with science and
end with a settlement.*

Keep showing your partner how much he/she means to you, even though you've been together for a while. Bring flowers, give a card, spend time together. It'll help you both stay happy and content as the years roll by!

Enjoy stillness together, for in stillness
love attains perfection.

Love is not passion.
Human love is reflection of divine love.
And God is perfect stillness.

Do something together. Consider volunteer work or even a household project. The idea is to accomplish something as a couple.

There is nothing holier in this life of ours than the first consciousness of love the first fluttering of its silken wings.

There comes a time when the soul of human beings, begin to faint for the atmosphere of affections they get to breathe.

Nobody is worth your tears and the one who is, will never make you cry.

*Love really has nothing to do with wisdom
or experience or logic. It is the
prevailing breeze in the land of youth.*

*Meet your Love after work at an elegant
bar or restaurant for a drink and
conversation about the day's events.*

Take a few hours each month to volunteer help together. Helping others makes you feel wonderful and helps you to bond. Soup kitchens, reading at old age homes etc. will bring you together in a special way.

68

*He who is intoxicated with wine will be sober
again in the course of the night, but he who
is intoxicated by the cupbearer will not
recover his senses until the day of judgment.*

*Love looks through a telescope;
envy, through a microscope.*

Familiarity breeds contempt.
When you stop treating your partner with love,
courtesy, and politeness, he or she may
feel contempt for you, and a lack of love.

Buy tickets for two to a sporting, cultural or entertainment event. Have a candle lit taligate party for just the two of you, before the event.

Don't be possessive. Reflect that no one ever truly owns another human being. Don't bind your beloved with the cord of your own needs. A plant flourishes when it is given free access to air and sunlight.

A great way to let your partner know you're thinking about them and love them:
Create a special signal that means, "I love you," such as a whistle. Or learn how to say "I love you" in sign language!
Then, when you're separated in a crowd, you can use your special signal and say, "I love you" without anyone else knowing.

Keep love in your heart. A life without it is like a sunless garden where the flowers are dead. The consciousness of loving and being loved brings a warmth and richness to life that nothing else can bring.

⁂

Hobby shows are everywhere. Whether it's a coin show, pet shown, gun show, or baseball card show, take your Love to one for the fun of it.

Those who have courage to love, also have the courage to suffer.

Speak more with the eyes "the windows of the soul." If you use your eyes when speaking, it will be as if those windows were framed with colourful curtains, making the home warm and inviting.

Never lose sight of the underlying reality of your love. Reflect: Isn't your long-term relationship more important than any passing disagreement? Flow with the longer rhythms of your love.

Sometimes you don't realize how much the daily grind of work and chores affect you until you get completely clear of it. Give yourself and your relationship that time to rest, recuperate and regain a sense of balance.

76

To say that you can love one person all your life is like saying that one candle will continue burning as long as you live.

A woman is more considerate in matters of love than a man.

When your spouse has hurt you in some way,
try not to lash out in anger. Instead,
by using language like 'I feel', to begin the
conversation, you allow him/her to be
receptive to you.
Anger builds walls, love breaks them down.

Love has no beginning nor any end, only an on-going ever-changing beauty of it's own.

Sit down with your Love and have a brainstorming session on ways to improve your relationship. Remember, no idea is a bad one, and you must keep an open mind.

When we communicate we need to discuss what we really want to happen to the relationship. We need to communicate what we are feeling and thinking.

80

Love is begun in time.
And over the passage of time is the proof.
Time qualifies the spark and fire of it.

଼ଔଔଔଔ

Did a woman ever love who would not give
all the years of tasteless serenity for one year,
for one month, for one day of
uncalculating love poured out upon the
man who returned it.

81

*Love is not only about looking deep
into each other's eyes,
but also about looking in the same direction.*

*One hour of love will teach a woman
more of her true relations than
all your philosophizing.*

&⚮&

*Love, which is only an episode in
the life of a man, is the sublime
history of a woman's life.*

Love is not in loving the perfect person,
it is in loving perfectly the imperfect person.

Love was to his impassioned soul,
not a mere part of its existence,
but the whole, the very life breath of his heart.

Love talks with better knowledge,
and knowledge with dearer love.

*Love bears all things, believes in all things,
hopes all things, endures all things.*

*Affections like the conscience, are rather to be
led than drawn; and it is to be feared,
they that marry where they do not love,
will love where they do not marry.*

*The wise want love; and those who
love, want wisdom.*

Some gifts simply last longer than others.
In reality the best gifts that we give aren't
necessarily material gifts.
They are gifts from the heart.

Keep a sense of humour.
Share together a sense of the absurd.
At the same time, be careful how you tease.
Never tease if the teasing is
unappreciated. Let your humour be kindly,
never sarcastic.

જ∞ાઉ

Love is a blend of informality and courtesy.
Courtesy is not diplomacy;
It is a mark of thoughtfulness and sensitivity.
Between two person who love each other,
courtesy is like a delicate waterfall, it keeps
the mountain pool of their love ever fresh.

89

Those who are faithful know the
trivial side of love; only the unfaithful
know it's tragic side.

Love is a wonder-One day it's perfect,
the next day it's even better.

Love means sharing the same road,
wherever it leads.

*Young men want to be faithful and are not,
old men want to be faithless but cannot.*

Be sure that you are not
excluding your soulmate because
of preconceptions others have convinced
you are very important.

Love looks at everyday
of life as something new.

Be creative while in a relationship.
Tend it as you tend plants in the garden,
sow the seeds when it's time,
water them and wait for the right season,
to see your garden filled with flowers.

*Love takes the meaning
in love's conference.*

*Love is a single soul
that dwells in two bodies.*

Absence makes the heart grow fonder.
It is like water upon fire;
a little, quickens; too much extinguishes it.

A heart is made gentle,
when it is full of love.

Love looks at everyday of
life as something new.

*Our first love
and last love is self-love.*

If love be blind,
love cannot hit the mark.

A faint heart never
won a fair lady.

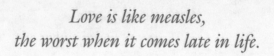

Love is like measles,
the worst when it comes late in life.

100

Men hate more steadily than they love.

Love, that comes too late,
Like a remorseful pardon slowly carried,
To the great sender turns a sour offence,
Crying, "That's good that's gone."

To love means to communicate to the other that you are all for him, that you will never fail or let him down when he needs you standing by him with all the encouragement.

When love begins to sicken and decay,
it useth an enforced ceremony.

Love is a babe; then might
I not say so, To give full growth
to that which still doth grow?

The greatest happiness in life is the conviction
that we are loved, loved for ourselves
or rather, loved in spite of ourselves.

A woman cannot love a man she feels to be
her inferior; love without veneration
and enthusiasm is only friendship.

Is love a tender thing?
It is too rough, too rude,
too boisterous; and it pricks like thorn.

*It is better to have loved and lost,
than not to love at all.*

Love is never lost.
If not reciprocated it will flow back
and soften and purify the heart.

Love is like the moon:
when it does not increase,
it decreases.

When having an argument with your spouse,
try not to win, but to compromise.
Keep away from the disagreements.

Love reckons hours for months,
and days for years;
and every little absence is an age.

Love, free as air, at sight of human ties,
Spreads its light wings,
and in a moment flies.

Hold hands together in silence.
You will learn to hear the
songs of love in silence.

*The supreme happiness of life
is the conviction that we are loved.*

*A lover without indiscretion
is no lover at all.*